Happy Mother's 💙 Day Mom

All My Love —
Sis

May 13, 2001

Mom, You're the Best!

Text copyright © 2001 by Harvest House Publishers
Eugene, OR 97402

ISBN 0-7369-0507-3

All works of art reproduced in this book are copyrighted by Susan Wheeler
and licensed by InterArt™ Licensing, Bloomington, IN, and may not be copied
or reproduced without permission. For more information regarding artwork
featured in this book, please contact:

> InterArt™ Licensing
> P.O. Box 4699
> Bloomington, IN 47402-4699
> 800-457-4045

Design and production by Garborg Design Works, Minneapolis, Minnesota

Harvest House Publishers has made every effort to trace the ownership of all
poems and quotes. In the event of a question arising from the use of a poem or
quote, we regret any error made and will be pleased to make the necessary
correction in future editions of this book.

Scripture quotations are taken from The Living Bible, Copyright © 1971 owned
by assignment by Illinois Bank N.A. (as trustee). Used by permission of
Tyndale House Publishers, Inc., Wheaton, Illinois 60189. All rights reserved.

Printed in Hong Kong.

01 02 03 04 05 06 07 08 09 10 /NG/ 10 9 8 7 6 5 4 3 2 1

Most of all the other beautiful things in life come by
twos and threes, by dozens and hundreds. Plenty of roses,
stars, sunsets, rainbows, brothers and sisters, aunts and
cousins, but only one mother in the whole world.

KATE DOUGLAS WIGGIN

My mother was an angel upon earth. She was a minister of blessing to all human beings within her sphere of action. She had no feelings but of kindness and beneficence, yet her mind was as firm as her temper was mild and gentle.

JOHN QUINCY ADAMS

"Mother" means selfless devotion, limitless sacrifices, and love that passes understanding.

AUTHOR UNKNOWN

From your parents you learn
love and laughter and how to
put one foot before the other.

HELEN HAYES

All you need in the world is love and laughter.
That's all anybody needs. To have love in one hand
and laughter in the other.

AUGUST WILSON

Beautiful as seemed

mama's face,

it became incomparably more

lovely when she smiled,

and seemed to enliven

everything about her.

LEO TOLSTOY

My mother drew a distinction between achievement and success. She said that "achievement is the knowledge that you have studied and worked hard and done the best that is in you.

Success is being praised by others, and that's nice, too, but not as important or satisfying. Always aim for achievement and forget about success."

HELEN HAYES

 Education commences at the mother's knee, and every word spoken within the hearing of little children tends towards the formation of character.

HOSEA BALLOU

A mother is not a person to lean on but
person to make leaning unnecessary.

DOROTHY FISHER

12

For I, too, was once a son,

tenderly loved by my mother

as an only child...

THE BOOK OF PROVERBS

There was a place in
childhood that I
remember well,
And there a voice of
sweetest tone bright
fairy tales did tell.

SAMUEL LOVER

Susan

13

For that's what a woman, a mother wants—to teach her children to take an interest in life. She knows it's safer for them to be interested in other people's happiness than to believe in their own.

MARGUERITE DURAS

When you are a mother you are never really alone in your thoughts. A mother always has to think twice, once for herself and once for her child.

SOPHIA LOREN

THERE IS NO
INFLUENCE SO
POWERFUL AS
THAT OF THE
MOTHER...

SARAH JOSEPH HALE

Mama was my
greatest teacher, a
teacher of compassion,
love and fearlessness.
If love is sweet as a
flower, then my
mother is that sweet
flower of love.

STEVIE WONDER

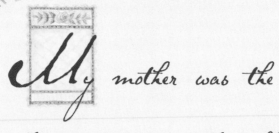

My mother was the influence in my life. She was strong; she had great faith in the ultimate triumph of justice and hard work.

JOHN H. JOHNSON

Mothers are the most

My very first lessons in the art of telling stories took
place in the kitchen... my mother and three or four
of her friends... told stories... with effortless art and
technique. They were natural-born storytellers...

PAULA MARSHALL

instinctive philosophers.

HARRIET BEECHER STOWE

The
mother's
heart is
the child's
schoolroom.

HENRY WARD BEECHER

SOMETIMES THE STRENGTH
OF MOTHERHOOD IS
GREATER THAN NATURAL LAWS.

BARBARA KINGSOLVER

It is not until you become a mother
that your judgment slowly turns to
compassion and understanding.

ERMA BOMBECK

The heart of a
mother is a
deep abyss
at the bottom
of which you
will always
discover
forgiveness.

HONORÉ DE BALZAC

It seems to me
that since I've
had children,
I've grown richer
and deeper.

ANNE TYLER

Susan

MY MOTHER WAS THE MOST BEAUTIFUL

WOMAN I EVER SAW. ALL I AM I OWE TO

MY MOTHER. I ATTRIBUTE ALL MY SUCCESS

IN LIFE TO THE MORAL,

INTELLECTUAL AND

PHYSICAL EDUCATION I

RECEIVED FROM HER.

GEORGE WASHINGTON

There is no friendship,
no love, like that of
the parent for the child.

HENRY WARD BEECHER

Marilla looked at her with a tenderness that would never have been suffered to reveal itself in any clearer light than that soft mingling of fire shine and shadow. The lesson of a love that should display itself easily in spoken word and open look was one Marilla could never learn. But she had learned to love this slim, gray-eyed girl with an affection all the deeper and stronger from its very undemonstrativeness. Her love made her afraid of being unduly indulgent, indeed. She had an uneasy feeling that it was rather sinful to set one's heart so intensely on any human creature as she had set hers on Anne, and perhaps she performed a sort of unconscious penance for this by being stricter and more critical than if the girl had been less dear to her. Certainly Anne herself had no idea how Marilla loved her.

L.M. MONTGOMERY
Anne of Green Gables

Mommy, I love you
For all that you do.
I'll kiss you and hug you
'Cause you love me, too.
You feed me and need me
To teach you to play,
So smile 'cause I love you
Every single day.

NICOLAS GORDON

Motherhood is the greatest
potential influence in human
society. Her caress first awakens
in the child a sense of security;
her kiss the first realization of
affection; her sympathy and
tenderness, the first assurance that
there is love in the world.

DAVID MCKAY

Her dignity consists in being unknown to the world; her glory is in the esteem of her husband; her pleasures in the happiness of her family.

JEAN ROUSSEAU

A mother is the truest friend we have, when trials, heavy and sudden, fall upon us; when adversity takes the place of prosperity; when friends who rejoice with us in our sunshine, desert us when troubles thicken around us, still will she cling to us, and endeavor by her kind precepts and counsels to dissipate the clouds of darkness, and cause peace to return to our hearts.

WASHINGTON IRVING

YOU'RE THE BEST
MOM IN THE WHOLE,
WIDE WORLD!

BEAVER CLEAVER

Youth fades;
love droops, the
leaves of friend-
ship fall; A
mother's secret
hope outlives
them all.

OLIVER WENDELL
HOLMES

To describe
my mother
would be to
write about a
hurricane in its
perfect power.

MAYA ANGELOU

My Mother: when my patience was at the end, hers had just begun.

DAVID WESLEY SOPER

A picture memory brings to me;

I look across the years and see

Myself beside my mother's knee.

I feel her gentle hand restrain

My selfish moods, and know again

A child's blind sense of wrong and pain.

But wiser now, a man gray grown,

My childhood's needs are better known.

My mother's chastening love I own.

JOHN GREENLEAF WHITTIER

A partnership with God
is motherhood.

AUTHOR UNKNOWN

Mother

Mother, how can I
begin to tell you all
that you mean to me?

You are the kind of
person that someday I
want to be.

You have given me
your very best; and I
want you now to know
that because of you my
life has been blessed;
and I love you so.

AUTHOR UNKNOWN

The noblest calling in the
world is that of mother.
True motherhood is the most
beautiful of all arts, the greatest
of all professions. She who
can paint a masterpiece or who
can write a book that will
influence millions deserves the
plaudits and admiration of
mankind; but she who rears
successfully a family of healthy,
beautiful sons and daughters
whose immortal souls will
be exerting an influence
throughout the ages long
after paintings shall have faded,
and books and statues shall
have been destroyed, deserves
the highest honor that man
can give.

DAVID MCKAY

The instruction received at the mother's knee, and the paternal lessons, together with the pious and sweet souvenirs of the fireside, are never effaced entirely from the soul.

ABBE FELICITE ROBERT DE LAMENNAIS

The mother love is like God's love; He loves us not because we are lovable, but because it is His nature to love, and because we are His children.

EARL RINEY

Maternal love:

A MIRACULOUS SUBSTANCE WHICH GOD MULTIPLIES AS HE DIVIDES IT.

VICTOR HUGO

GOD PARDONS LIKE A MOTHER WHO KISSES THE OFFENSE INTO EVERLASTING FORGETFULNESS.

HENRY WARD BEECHER

The sweetest sounds
to mortals given
Are heard in Mother,
Home and Heaven.

WILLIAM GOLDSMITH BROWN

No man is poor who has had a godly mother.

ABRAHAM LINCOLN

Best friends forever mom and me,

picking flowers and climbing trees.

A shoulder to cry on, secrets to share—

Warm hearts and hands that really care.

AUTHOR UNKNOWN

WHO RAN TO HELP ME

WHEN I FELL,

AND WOULD SOME

PRETTY STORY TELL,

OR KISS THE PLACE AND MAKE IT WELL?

My Mother.

ANN TAYLOR

Never a sigh for the cares
that she bore for me,
Never a thought of the
joys that flew by;
Her one regret that she
couldn't do more for me,
Thoughtless and selfish,
her Master was I.

Oh, the long nights that
she came at my call to me!
Oh, the soft touch of her
hands on my brow!
Oh, the long years that she
gave up her all to me!
Oh, how I yearn for her
gentleness now!

Slave to her baby! Yes,
that was the way of her,
Counting her greatest
of services small;
Words cannot tell what this
old heart would say of her,
Mother—the sweetest and
fairest of all.

EDGAR GUEST

Women know
The way to rear up
children (to be just)
They know a simple,
merry, tender knack
Of tying sashes,
fitting baby-shoes
And stringing
pretty words that
make no sense.

ELIZABETH BARRETT
BROWNING

Mother's love is peace.
It need not be acquired,
it need not be deserved.

ERICH FROMM

41

I think true mothers everywhere
Are gently brushed by angel wings
And in some stillness hear God speak,
"Your child can do great things!"
And so a mother dreams her dreams,
And has the love to see
In every struggling, stumbling child
What God knows he can be!
How can I fail to seek His will,
And follow in His way —
When I have known my mother's prayers
Lifting me up each day?

EMILY SARGENT

A mother is a person who seeing there are only four pieces of pie
for five people, promptly announces she never did care for pie.

TENNEVA JORDAN

Mothers hold their children's hands for a while...their hearts forever.

AUTHOR UNKNOWN

You may have tangible wealth untold;
Caskets of jewels and coffers of gold.
Richer than I you can never be —
I had a mother who read to me.

STRICKLAND GILLILAN

God made a wonderful mother,

A mother who never grows old;

He made her smile of the sunshine,

And He molded her heart of pure gold;

In her eyes He placed bright shining stars,

In her cheeks fair roses you see;

God made a wonderful mother,

And He gave that dear mother to me.

PAT O'REILLY

46

"**M**" is for the million things she gave me,

"**O**" means only that she's growing old,

"**T**" is for the tears she shed to save me,

"**H**" is for her heart of purest gold;

"**E**" is for her eyes, with love-light shining,

"**R**" means right, and right she'll always be,

Put them all together, they spell "**Mother,**" A word that means the world to me.

HOWARD
JOHNSON

A mother's love is the fuel that enables a
normal human being to do the impossible.

AUTHOR UNKNOWN